Daphne Lifts Up

poems by

Donna L. Emerson

Finishing Line Press
Georgetown, Kentucky

Daphne Lifts Up

Dedicated to Virginia Dorris, friend and second mother

Additional Praise for *Daphne Lifts Up*

Donna Emerson is an extraordinary poet of ordinary life, revealing intimate details of her and her family's relationships. Her poems are intensely personal, yet resonate with us all. The language is spattered with color; music, art, and nature trigger emotions throughout. It's a collection of recent poems and some of her best work over a number of years. "She Lay Asleep Wearing Oxygen" recounts the scene during Emerson's mother's passing, told with a seasoned reporter's feel for detail and the power of an accomplished poet's craft.

Geoffrey Link, Editor and Publisher of the San Francisco Study Center Press

Grounded firmly in the realm of human relationships, Donna Emerson's powerfully personal poems bring us into the life of the heart and heat-held memory, offering intimate depictions of a world alive with family and friends. Of her several poems about her mother, "She Lay Asleep Wearing Oxygen" is an especially poignant account of her mother's final illness and death. While wisely reminding us that loss waits at the last shore of love, the poems of *Daphne Lifts Up* vividly celebrate a life of enduring connections.

Elizabeth C. Herron, Phd, Sonoma County Poet Laureate, 2022-2024, author of *In the Cities of Sleep*.

Copyright © 2025 by Donna L. Emerson
ISBN 979-8-89990-071-6 First Edition
All rights reserved under International and Pan-American Copyright Conventions. No part of this book may be reproduced in any manner whatsoever without written permission from the publisher, except in the case of brief quotations embodied in critical articles and reviews.

ACKNOWLEDGMENTS

Please see pages 83-84 for a full list of prior publications of poems and awards in this collection. A special thank you to editors who share my love of the written word, its power to inspire and heal.

Publisher: Leah Huete de Maines

Editor: Christen Kincaid

Cover Art: Barbara Ann Marlin, Watercolor, "Daphne"

Cover Photo: Donna Emerson

Author Photo: Dennis Davis

Cover Graphics: Elizabeth Maines McCleavy

Order online: www.finishinglinepress.com
                also available on amazon.com

Author inquiries and mail orders:
Finishing Line Press
PO Box 1626
Georgetown, Kentucky 40324
USA

Contents

Comforts
Hummingbird Couple 1
After Winter Rains 2
Skimming the Water 3
I Was Raised on Love 4
Longberries 5
Mildred Belle 6
At Four and Thirty 7
Rhapsody and Boogie-Woogie 8
A Boy Named Ned 10
Living Language 11
Neighbors 12
Vernal Sap 14
Mystery of the Boil 15

Dark and Light
In the Dark 19
Spring Wind 20
Long Distance 21
Canada Goose Nesting 22
Juliet Belle 23
Ask Her 24
Bonnie 25
In the Retelling 26
A Day's Work 27

Daphne Lifts Up
What Hollyhocks Can Do 31
Gustav Klimt 32
Unraveling 33
For Mary, *Sotto Voce* 34
Awakening 35
In the Middle of a Long Marriage 36
Before AIDS Was a Word 37
On the Lakeshore Limited 39
Before Mother Died 40

Listening to *L'Isle Joyeuse* 41
Daphne Lifts Up... 42

Gathering and Letting Go
Alone 45
Hello and Good-bye in Athens.. 46
In Friendship: Anais Nin 47
Objects Found... 50
Swimming with Swallowtail.. 51
Heroics 53
She Lay Asleep Wearing Oxygen 55
Sarah Mae 61
Nine Years After Mom Died.. 62
Old Faithful 63
Reunion: Winter Visit, Family Homestead 65
On the Plaza, Santa Fe 67
In the Blue Room.. 68
Lampyridae.. 69
The Changing Season... 70
Virginia and Juliet 72
Porcelain Cups in the Sun 73
Birdsong... 74
Blood Appears... 75
Enter Autumn 76
Inside and Out 77
What I Want to Know.. 79
The Dascomb Aerie 80
The Cows on Our Street 81
Belting Out Beethoven... 82

Acknowledgments 85
Biography... 87

Comforts

Hummingbird Couple

The pearl grey hummingbird
wings aflutter
body still as a bullet

at eye level,
three feet
from my astonishment

same time
as yesterday.

She spies pink blouse,
vanishes, a sharp
right turn.

Her mate
repeats her visit,
red throat bobs at my eyes.

I would give him
my shirt,
rip it off in pieces

just his size
if he would
only stay.

After Winter Rains

Walking the burned earth behind Hannah's house
after the Santa Rosa fires, after soaking rain,
I see a buckeye thrust
its pippin shoots straight up, as if to say
"Here I am!"
right beside the black, burned trunk
of its mother tree.

Its closed leaflets, yellow-green at first,
open wide like a hand spreading its fingers
eager for fresh air, sun, and rain.

Then come flowers that grow only after fire.
Baker's globe mallow with its rose-purple color
holds seeds needing fire to germinate.
They can wait up to a hundred years, dormant,
before bursting into blooms.
Sundry stamens radiating from a long tube
command us to stop and savor.

I need to walk our hillsides of new poppies,
purple Canterbury bells, monkeyflower, ceanothus,
scarlet larkspur. They give us carpet,
colors to satisfy the eye, irrepressible
life beyond wildfire.

Skimming the Water

This morning I swim laps, startle to a stop when bird wings shudder overhead. Looking up, a flock of squawking Canada Geese. *So like Mother,* I say aloud.

I ran alongside such a skein, the morning she died. Late fall in Ohio, cold. They honked for five minutes, me feeling their ruckus in my shoulders, sensing mom's spirit flying away with them.

They skimmed the pond across from her house. I ran beside, then under them until I ran out of breath, blinking hot tears on chilling skin. Next to a frozen field of dried corn stalks, rattling.

Today, draped across the lane line in the blue pool, I cry for her leaving, her open talking to her sisters, all of them together, these thirty years of missing her.

I Was Raised on Love

> *Sharon Olds says in* Father, *that if she'd been raised on love she wouldn't have felt such disdain for her father.*

I was raised by a loving man.
He was rarely there.
He stood behind aloof, duty, *gotta* go.

While he died I held tight to his love,
spit out his untamed names for despair,
reached through stiff percale for his hands,
last words, a blessing.

But we had formal conversations.
He spoke of his oat cell cancer, his funeral,
pain, said he was not afraid, just wanted
the nurse with the pills.

He thought the man in the next room
had died and no one came to check,
asked me to look, insisted that it be now.
I stepped next door, found a dead man,
his wife and priest in prayer,
told Dad the man was with his wife, safe.

I expected it to end there.
Accepted that it was enough
for me to love him, hold his hand,
share silence.

His hands were still alive, well formed,
confident, long fingered, gentle.
Had we held hands in our life twice?
Slowly he squeezed my hand and said,
"We'll get through this, honey."

I cried open mouthed now,
saying my name for him in childhood,
the father I'd hoped to see
up close, someday.

Longberries

We rode the horses toward the pines through open meadows,
tickling oats, glad for no trail in July. Local hunters bend
all the grasses in October when we are not here.

Grandfather was looking for something.
I followed amiably, sun soaking my arms and ankles.
"Here we are," he pulled up his reins. "Today we pick longberries."

As I jumped down, Grandpa handed me a kitchen pot.
Showed me how to push my belt through its handle so both hands were free.
He waded in. I stood back aways.

Compact bushes clumped under a young maple sapling.
Fat green leaves, prickers pointing at me. *Glad I have my overalls on. Wish I had gloves. I will go home all scratched tonight.*

Grandpa walked straight to the middle. "These are not blackberries. Put your fingers all the way around the berry, to where it meets its stem and pull very gently."

How long they were, some the length of my little finger. Juicy and only sweet, soft and furry outside, bursting to sugar-wet centers. No rough spots, no sour-then-sweet like the common blackberry we'd picked before.

Long-lasting.
Forgetting the stickers, I pushed deeper into the bush.

Grandpa threw me a wadded-up shirt to cover my bleeding arms.
Then I could pick to my heart's delight.
Berry on berry, my pot filling fast. *Pies tonight!*

Mildred Belle

I miss her, her fleshy arms.
She never talked diets.
She baked breads and cakes
from scratch, instead. Taught me
to churn butter and cheese.

She never wore make-up.
Her stockings rolled just above the knee,
black lace-up shoes below.
She wore full aprons over nylon dresses.

Her hair strawberry blond,
in a farm-style French twist,
loose, then gray, then white.
And freckles everywhere.

She spoke Tennyson and Frost
from memory when these fit
the moment, told family stories,
like the time she whacked
Uncle James in the head with a log
meant for the wood stove, calling
him *a mean, mean man.*

She knew all the names
of the Black Panthers
in the sixties, and exactly
where McNamara went wrong.

She never hit me.
She never screamed at me.
Her entrances were quiet.
She was listening.

At Four and Thirty

My father at thirty, young, strong, with clear blue eyes, a spring in every step, strode into the sun room in Cleveland singing, "Zippedy do-dah, zippedy aye..." my oh my, what a wonderful day... Perfect pitch. He lifted me onto his lap and sang the rest. I think his shirt was off. It was summer. "Plenty of sunshine comin' my way..."

I marveled then at how handsome he was. I knew he carried it with him, full of youth. I reflected his happiness. I was lucky to see him this day, without my younger brother and sister around.

In this same spirit he taught me to play chess, to swim all the strokes. He bought me white water wings and stood beside me at Lake Isabella, teaching me to float above my fear. He stood in a swimming pool for half an hour until I had the nerve to dive in. He tutored my algebra when I didn't care how much longer it took Ted to row upriver than Tom.

Over years, worn down by his chosen life of hard work, he no longer sang. Began drinking martinis at lunch and before dinner with one of the many moves for his career advancement. He fell asleep in his green recliner. We shared few words or laughter. I knew where that young man had gone. Seen his pressing ambition flourish and flower, the many moves to new cities, new schools for us kids, new upwardly mobile job titles like Sales Manager, Vice-President, President. Heard his night arguments with Mother, the drunken dancing with other women, the silence when Mom slapped him at five in the morning. And left.

I wanted her to stay away. See if my father could miss her, find deeper streams inside, songs that he could care to sing for her and with her, make him sing the way he sang that morning in cathedrals of sunlight, when I was four.

Rhapsody and Boogie-Woogie

Mother played Rachmaninoff's "Rhapsody on a Theme of Paganini"
some afternoons. "Claire de Lune" and "Deep Purple" came next.
Unless she felt wild and wiggled into boogie-woogie.

I sat in another room, open-mouthed at her virtuosity.
She played as if she knew every measure from birth.
Her crescendo perfectly timed, not sliding off the page,
slender wrists rising for delicate phrasing.

She swayed and sang with Hoagy Carmichael.
Understood the long arc of these many-faceted pieces,
loved the swing of modern sounds.

Her discipline caused me to stop reading
I fell into the sounds and moods she made.

In life as an overwhelmed young mother, husband away on business,
she became short-tempered, abrupt, out of control with her children.

At the keyboard she floated, soared, serene, like a reed in a stream,
grabbed at just the right times, tenderly embraced chords at others.

When she taught me to play at five,
I stumbled and she slapped my hands.
I still wanted to play like she played.
Played better when I had a teacher.

At thirteen, when my teacher moved away
she never found another.

Mother suddenly died, still young.
She left me her Baldwin spinet.
I had it shipped to me in California.

Sons and daughter learned to play.
Years later, I consider piano lessons again.
Are my hands nimble enough to advance
through the circle of fifths?

To play her music. Make it my music. To master sonata, roll with boogie-woogie. Next to Chopin and Mozart. Beethoven and Elvis in the bench.

A Boy Named Ned

At fourteen, I had a first boyfriend named Ned.
Just like Nancy Drew.
He smiled at me and called me after school.
We talked for an hour on the telephone
or until his mother or baseball called him away.
He had a lovely rounded head with ample brown hair
and eyes that looked into forever. I was part of forever.

He gave me his ring. It was big and heavy.
It meant we were going steady.
I had to buy a heavy enough chain to hold it,
costing more than my allowance.
After a few weeks I wondered.
Ned didn't talk as much as before and his dance
was a slow walk that made my hip hurt.

I liked when we played "52 Switch" at Judy's party.
"Spin the Bottle" exciting but I was glad it was dark.
Last week in my daughter's sociology class I learned
modern dating rituals exist so you don't have to commit.

Perhaps I knew that at fourteen and gave the ring back to Ned.
And George asked me to be his partner in all the dances,
even the polka, at the eighth grade dance.
Ned soon dated Ellen and they got married five years later.
They moved toward forever. I went to California.

Forty years later Ellen died, complications of diabetes.
Ned called me yesterday about his brain cancer.
I think he called me because I knew about not forever.
He called me Honey. I told him I remembered everything.

Living Language

He told me not to use Latin in my poem,
that only a few people are interested.
Plain American words are good enough
and you get the meaning faster.

But I love Latin, the original names of flowers
and trees, even music, like when we sang
the Bach *Magnificat* or the *B Minor Mass*
in the Grace Cathedral. Breathing so much
air, I felt the columns move.

For four years in high school each of us
had to stand beside our chairs to translate.

One autumn day, my Latin teacher, Mrs. Carfagno,
usually so buttoned up, with her tight
strawberry-blond curls turning grey,
shouted out: "Gaudeamus Igitur,
Juvenes dum sumus!"
Then we all stood up in the front of the classroom
and sang all the verses with her. Her face flushed red.

Right in the middle of Cicero. Before Julius Caesar
crossed the Rubicon. Even before we learned
"Alea iacta est!" the die was cast.
Latin, engraved into me, forever.

Neighbors

He hasn't put his baseball cap back on. Wally wants to stay longer. His blue eyes linger. At eighty-six, he walked the half mile to our house. He has things to say. I wait.

A moment for his snow-white hair, the crew cut he's always worn. Hair growing in straight rows like the barley he's sown. His square farmer's hands stand out, even while resting on the armchair by the fire. Muscular arms and fingers still steady, though mottled—his heart condition.

After the spell when his heart almost stopped, he talks more often.

We used to run through all the rooms of your grandmother's house. Her doors always open, even when they were out. Back then, we all left our doors open. We ran up and down the stairs. In and out, my brothers and me.

Did you know there was a dumbwaiter in the kitchen? She used to draw it up to the second floor, put the clothes in, then drop it down to the basement to wash. She'd pull it up again to the kitchen to take the clothes out to dry on the clothesline.

I've never heard this before. I can see her tossing upstairs sheets in her long white dress. Only told by Grandma that she and Uncle Forrest used to play in the dumbwaiters of the big Victorians her father'd built on Liberty Street.

"I saw that ladder-like wood attached to the kitchen wall behind the gas stove. Painted yellow like the wall. Never knew it used to be a dumbwaiter!"

Wally talks of the fire in 1974 that burned Grandma's big farmhouse to the ground.

Someone came barreling down the road and woke me up toward morning. I called the fire department but it was too late. We ran up to see. Fire chief said must've been faulty wiring in the basement. Nobody took care of it much after your grandfather died.

I say: "See that space on the wall? The picture I just took of you will hang right there. You've always been part of our family."

Yep. He likes that.

Wally told me last time that his mother, always sick, died before he reached ten. He's the last one of that generation, can hardly walk to his mailbox some days. Can't hunt any more, keeps his shotgun near the front door to scare the red squirrels. Calls me in California to tell me about all the walnuts they've packed into every opening in his trees.

Vernal Sap

We run with our pails to the sugar maples.
Marked last summer, when leaves were easy
to read, tree crowns high and wide.
Daughter taps the spile in place
midst several versions of *ahh*
as clear sap drips out.

We discover an unexpected bush of sugar maples
across the road from the original trees.
Their seedlings must have blown straight across the road,
so that nine young trees stand equidistant,
most too young yet to tap.

In a day, fifteen trees are tapped, named, embraced
for their beauty and life force, given freely to us,
as long as we protect them from harm.

As did my mother, uncles, grandparents
and great grandparents
over the last two hundred years, in these woods.

This marks the start of Spring,
when we see water flow for the first time, under the ice
on the road.

Daughter finishes her work, hugs the tree
and names it "Eldest Granddaughter."

The gushing older tree by the old farmhouse
we name "Grandmother." Her bark thick,
scarred, lumpy in spots like a darned sock,
holds a frozen bit of sap where a vertical,
waist-high crevice sits.
It must have access to her heartwood.

Mystery of the Boil

We boil sugar maple sap in our old fire pit in the open.
For hours sweet steam wafts around our bodies,
smoke around our feet.

Half a day passes while we feed the fire and stir
what feels like only water. One of us stirring,
one or two gathering wood from the woods.
Locust is the most dense, lasts the longest.

The ten gallon pot sustains a rolling boil,
reducing liquid to a gallon. Then comes
the caramel-colored sap we filter
through cheesecloth into small pots.

Stories emerge, of how grandpa did these
same things in the woods with the horses.
Or the year they made a sugar shack,
freezing outdoors in late January.

Then we move to the kitchen stove for the measuring
and final boil, anticipation rising with the temperature.

We wait again. As sap becomes more viscous.
our thermometer slowly climbs
to seven degrees above boiling. Slippery bubbles appear
and we shout out loud, just before the pot boils over:
Real maple syrup!

We fill funnels placed in glass bottles. Thick amber liquid
settles. We cap and lay the hot bottles on their sides,
watch bubbles disperse. Near midnight we can,
but for excitement, rest.

Dark and Light

In the Dark

Stay out. Don't come in here.
His voice a vice, sharp, cold.

I had glimpsed enough edges
to see he was slaughtering
a deer. No lights on. A four-paned
window over his left shoulder.
He stood behind a four-footed
animal, used something sharp
again and again.

I wanted to think
he was currying a horse
but this shadowed shape
smaller, more delicate.

A terrible smell of rotten
something came from the barn.
It slid into my nostrils
And wouldn't come out.

How could he be doing that
in the place where the horses
slept and ate their breakfast?

Spring Wind

As we nestle in the old bed,
the one my grandparents
slept in, their same room,
we speak to the dark
about all that has changed.

…feels like the thirties,
you say, looking straight up.
When liberal democracy
was in serious question.
When a small man, Adolph, crawled
out of his World War I foxhole
telling Germans to realize
their nationalism, reclaim it,
conquer in its name, lie to make
it superior, withdraw from the world.

Seasonal spring wind blows through
the cherry tree into our screens,
then over our bed. My flesh chills.

How many of us remember? I say.
Pull up Aunt Liva's quilt and turn over.
Stone cold, unsettled, in a horsehair bed.

Long Distance

When I miscarried at home, the doctor was away. We spoke by telephone. "Blighted Ovum" he said. "One in five."

We hadn't told my two-year-old son, but while I was in the bathroom, becoming an animal, trying to keep the baby inside, he stood outside the door crying, saying *I hope Mommy doesn't lose the baby.*

He hadn't been told. How did he know?

My mother didn't answer when I called. My best friend was away. I called my sister, who listened quietly at first. That deep silence on long telephone wires.

She said, *Can you think of some reason for this to happen?* I said no, feeling as if I were falling into a dark cave. I told her what the doctor had said.

I mean, could there be some flaw in you that you need to face? Something that you should change right now?

What? I crawled to the surface.

My puzzlement finally turned to self-protection: *You know, I don't find this helpful right now. Let's talk another time.* I hung up the phone.

I couldn't find a dictionary. Blight comes from nature doesn't it? A blighted tree, Like an act of God. Was that what he was saying? I liked that much better.

I dialed my mother again, who answered. We wept.

Canada Goose Nesting

She straddles her eggs
like a child in pajamas
crouching over a floor heater
as winter lingers.

One webbed foot tucked
under an egg so large
it sticks out the back

until she puffs out her podgy
chest. Her body and feathers
loom larger.

Down she glides,
covering the entire top
of her three-feet-across twiggy
nest, where six sizable eggs rest
secure. Warm in the wind.

I think of Juliet nursing—

latching on my nipple
until the seal is complete,
open mouth against areola

or me sitting down
on you spread out—
until it feels like home.

But oh, she's up again
turning over an egg.
What made her decide
it wasn't quite right?

Juliet Belle

I've lost the names of days,
their assigned numbers.
Yet fluttering birds sing

in the chimney at dawn,
winter clouds turn pink
at first and last light.

I live in the rhythm of new life,
baby hunger and satiation.
Perched on my heart,
latched on my breast,

keen observer of her world.
She thrusts upon us, unblinking
soft rhymes of wonder and fresh hope.

Ask Her

after William Shakespeare

My daughter's eyes are nothing like the moon.
Palest blue of ancient teacups, undisguised,
within our home's foundation, a night in June.
If brows be perfect, hers, more perfect, lie.
Near rippling hair that hangs full down unfastened,
shimmers sun and sun's reflections linger
across shoulders soft as swan-down, ask her,
she'll laugh, tell stories running, all aglimmer.
I have seen fillies frolic like this one.
Muscle and bone form her exquisite leap.
But few turn back to laugh and sing in fun
while learning Latin, conjugating Greek.

Though not yet grown, advanced in speech
With harmony and grace painted on her feet.

Bonnie

When I think of Nelson Mandela I see Bonnie Rogers
sitting next to me, in McIntyre School's second grade,
her face the color of strong coffee with a splash of cream,
smiling bigger than the Susquehanna.

Her freckles on her nose just like his.

She taught me to suck my arm on the inside of my elbow.
It made a red mark. *You'll both get cancer,*
her grandma said.

I took her home from school, where my mother
wouldn't speak to me the entire afternoon, snapped
at us both in the kitchen, wouldn't look at me except
with hard slate eyes, like the witch in Snow White.

When Bonnie left, Mother smacked me
down, told me *never bring that picaninny here, again.*
Why?
  Because she's poor.
We're poor too.

I told Bonnie the next day that my mother wouldn't
let her come home with me anymore.
Bonnie and her cousin Irene called me a fool.

When Nelson Mandela got out of prison and stood
with his arms outstretched around all of Africa,
I hoped Bonnie was watching.

And when he died last week I imagined
we both were crying for all the people
who didn't get to know each other.

In the Retelling

I dream of yellow-orange flames, flashing through pine trees.

Stifling smoke startles me awake. *I don't hear a smoke alarm.*
I bolt up, grab my crutches my fifth night after knee surgery,
drag my new leg to the back door. Sickly yellow light through the house.
I can't make out flames through the ochre off-color haze outdoors.
But seeing our trees bent back by strong north wind, choking on smoke,
I slam the door shut. *Big fire blowing south*, I say. The clock says 2:30 am.

I cannot rouse my husband, who also dreaming says—*Bad time for a fire*—.
I stumble to my sick room, the house now in ghostly light, all the usual
shapes not themselves. In scattered shadows I misstep, fall against
the heavy bed frame, my head hitting the headboard. I lie on the floor, confused.

Get up, this is a serious fire, I shout toward my husband. I turn on the television. Fire everywhere, jumping roads, even the freeway: Fountain Grove, Bennett Valley, Coffey Park. No warnings. People running, screaming. But the fire outruns them. Cars blocked by fire. Hospitals emptying. *Petalumans, prepare to evacuate*, my phone beeps. That's us.
We pack up family photographs, the Emerson Bible, the Roseville vase
Dad never let us touch, silver baby shoes, Mother's and Grandmother's journals, my own. What of those thousands of people who have not even a minute to take one piece of clothing?

Our house does not burn. We cough on smoke, wear face masks for weeks. My asthma requires triple medications, my leg slowly heals. I can't get out to help except hold the hands of those who need to talk, rage, fall apart with a witness. Sometimes recovery is in the retelling.

The carpet man spent an hour extra yesterday showing me a photo of his old house in Coffey Park and then his black, barren, empty plot after the October fire. His wife awakened at 1:50 a.m. to see their garage and all trees outside, ablaze. They left at 2 am October 8 with their three-year old, two cats, two Rottweilers. No hotel would take them. They drove to his buddy's in Salinas. Last, he showed me his new two-story house as if it were a new child, just built in the same spot as the old.
It's all about insurance, he says. Sometimes recovery is the re-building, proving you're still alive, that you saved yourself.

A Day's Work

The doctor and nurse call the social worker.
"Help us get her to leave," they say.

The social worker sits on a couch too low for her legs
so her eyes can meet the drowning eyes of the woman,
the small thin woman with long hair like Ophelia.

"Can you help me?" Ophelia pleads.
"I don't know if I can, but I'd like to."

Ophelia talks of the night before:

Her four month old baby boy sound asleep,
healthy, safe, pink. Winding her hair into her fist
the young mother speaks about the crib,
where she got it, the sheets,
the air temperature, the way he lay,
the way she always tucks him in,
always made him lay, his round downy head,
just sprouting hair, blond hair, her hair,

every step to his room, her sleepy footsteps
on the rug to the spot where her baby stopped breathing.
Every thought she had before and at that lurching
moment of discovery,
her frozen screams louder than jungle birds wounded
in ambush, just as she screams now, falls on the taller woman,
pounds on her back, drags herself down the blouse and skirt
to the floor beside the other's feet.

"Tell me I didn't do this,"
"You didn't do this."
"They want me to go home. I can't go home."

The taller woman slips to the floor beside Ophelia,
tears slipping down her cheekbones.

"Of course you can't go home. Your baby is here. You must stay
with your baby, he's still your baby. They can't take him away from

you."

The social worker thinks about her own son, taking all the blankets off his bed, as she strokes the younger mother's hair.
Then they walk to find the infant boy.

Daphne Lifts Up

What Hollyhocks Can Do

She plants hollyhocks.
Each stalk grows tall, taller,
climbing up her house,
up the windows, toward the roof.

All these strong stems
boast blues, yellows, pinks.

I grow buoyant to see them
like a trumpet
in a brass choir.

I hear her singing,
flowers in each room,
bunches like those held
by the balloon man at the fair.

Gustav Klimt

During my mid-twenties a boy gave me
a postcard of Klimt's painting, "The Kiss."
That boy had curly black hair like Gustav Klimt.
Like the swarthy man in Klimt's painting,
he held me strong, He loved women like the painter.
And I knew we would never wed or be partners
beyond our current victory.

In today's exhibit at the Legion of Honor,
a life-size photograph: Klimt wears an old painter's
smock with likely nothing underneath.
I'm sure he hasn't bathed. His feral hair
and beard look tossed by wind.

He looks at the camera as if caught slightly unawares,
meeting the lens but sharing little about himself.
Perhaps a wink. He's on his way to paint.
Then make love to his model. I still want to be
one of them.

Never married, he fathered fourteen children, filled
the world with the frank beauty of the female body.

Unraveling

I am trying to accept that we simply grew up on each other. Brown eyes dancing, blue eyes watching.

Your bulky frame in junior high. I leaned against the chain link fence at Edgewood on your first day of school as you laughed hard, and leaned over. Were you about to slap your knee? Almost as if you were happy. Yet stiff.

We rode the same school bus. Sam drove it. We were in classes every day. You gave smart answers. I liked your long eyelashes, your mother's confidence, your father's smile, the way you pressed me against you later dancing, the way our bodies fit in the dance. We didn't sit on the swing on the porch. We kissed but didn't know which way to go. You came for me when I was with Charles, I came running for you when you walked away with Betty. You laughed and bent over. I laughed with you.

You asked me to wait for you after I moved to Ohio. I said of course not, we were not enough alike, you were an only child. Then wept for a day, not knowing why, as your car tires met the crushed gravel of my driveway. Why couldn't you stay longer? I was there but didn't know it. Laughing through you. Why did you read *Catch-22* in Berkeley when you came to see me? I sat next to you wondering why you weren't talking to me. We couldn't open wider.

You went away on a ship, later locked up in Stroudsburg, never to leave. You stayed inland, I spread on the coast.

At the high school reunion you lied, "…always friends …always enjoy time with you." More important than friends. You didn't lie at the reunion, "…still a guy who doesn't know himself very well…" still leaning and laughing. Why am I still watching?

We may dance again. I will feel the pull as my breast folds into your chest. But you will not pull me closer. You'll say to yourself, "What good would that do?" You will prevail. Perhaps that is resolution.

For Mary, *Sotto Voce*

Mary Cassatt painted mothers
as monuments,
well-nourished, flourishing
with their babies, with themselves,
at the bath, in the nursery, kitchen,
at the opera, on lawns.

They wore white, carried fans
or parasols, the more white the better,
white touched with blue paint
to make the white whiter.

Mary lets us come close
to her world of women.

I want to touch arms, red-blond hair,
take the baby onto my lap, take tea.
I want to watch the opera next to her
and say *thank you, Mary, you know
and show the world full women.*

You said you wanted to *be someone, not something.*
Even more than yourself,
you gave me back to myself as well.

Awakening

Wake me with your fluttering eyelashes on my eyelids.
Tap lavender stems on my wrists.
Curve and tip my fingernails pink.

Paint my fence pure white.
Fill in my windows with stained glass, colors of Louis Tiffany.
While you're at it, won't you make a big skylight above my bed?
Open the attic windows at the tops of the cupola.
Watch the doves fly out, spread the morning open with their wings.

Notice the white lace at the top of my socks, tips touching my ankles.
And the white lace at the kitchen window.

Sing cradle songs outside my bath.
Wait for the mockingbird to best you.

Play cello among my mother's zinnias.
She will hear you.
Talk to me about the spiritual interior of words.

You can play piano duets with my mother while I rest.

And as I rock the baby, listen to her laugh.

Watch her reach up and touch my face,
walk up my chest to my neck with her long toes
sucking and smiles, all at once.

In the Middle of a Long Marriage

Turn this embrace to magic while you may.
We both know we have spent what was ours
long ago while clouds decayed.

You with your held back passion-flower
me with my dreams of a perfect man.
We can only meet in darkness and pretend.

You hold out hopes of meeting me again.
I find comfort in meeting less, my friend.

Still we plan, go to Corinth and its shore
travel the inside passage, pay and delay,

spend more, buy more, eat more, what for?
Promise and sweet talk, new vows, no floor.

None of these can help us stay or go,
only deep-within change, neither of us allow.

Before AIDS Was a Word

My new client looks like a ranch
hand, skin taut, bowlegged,
hands smell of leather.

The doctor thought it a *passing flu*.
Now he's *infected with some virus,*
our town does not yet know.

Smells like chemicals,
lies in bed all day.
He's becoming someone else.

He presses himself into the farthest
corner of this cold room
as if he can't stand to see me.

Turns his blotched face away
if I edge closer.
His skin stretched thin over bones
like buckskin with bullet holes.

I wonder if I have to worry
about catching what he has.
His creased brow's more worried
than my wondering.

His voice breathes heavy,
lost its low notes last month.
He seethes in his throat
with each exhalation.

He begged a room
from his sister on her old sheep ranch.
She isn't sure. Has young kids.

His sickness balled up like bad news
in the bottom of their basement.
No one climbs down there.

I look beyond his head, outside his room
to the new lamb—white wool against green
field, the ewe mother ignores.

I ask about his relationships.
"It's all past."

For his illness a blanket full of holes
which covers, does not warm him.

On the Lakeshore Limited

Leaves of my childhood trees lean toward us.
From arching old trunks, they look large
enough to happily swallow us up.
Or brush all over us, up and down, urge away
city smog and dirt,
remnants from the other world.

Oaks and maples sweep us clean, sumac and elm
flutter away extra water. Pink clover lies in a green carpet,
from the silver train we ride to the horizon.

Corn just ankle high today, beans in bunches,
rows, a half mile long and straight.
What began as the Hudson to the west,
now the Mohawk River flows parallel to train tracks
with dams near the old bridges.

Old Indian settlement names call out to us: Sonyea, Painted Post,
Cohocton, Avoca, Kanona, Lake Canandaigua, Lake Conesus,
where the torches are still passed once a year.

June, O June, you welcome us home.

Before Mother Died

She said, *pack up my boxes, put them in the basement or attic.*
Then they'll be taken away.

Mom, your boxes are still in my basement.
They've sat there for thirty years,
next to the old bookshelves.

I think of them there at night.
Sometimes I get up, go to them to remove dust and cobwebs.

They settle back in, in their spot where the cats sleep.
I notice they're often warm,
the cats like them too.

Every few months I find myself opening the smaller box.
The one with your letters, poems, your journals.

Out fly your best words, the light, lilting ones
the ones we saw most on paper, your funny stories,
the poems you and Grandma sent back and forth.

I read and cry and laugh out loud.
Once I even brought a blanket for the floor,
lay there with your paragraphs and stanzas until the cats got hungry.

I felt flushed, head to toe, like I did when I read *Black Beauty*
warm by the heater in our house in Pennsylvania before school,
while you made scrambled eggs in the kitchen.

We won't be carrying these boxes away.
They protect the foundation of the house.

Listening to *L'Isle Joyeuse*

by Claude Debussy

His grace notes lead me to the herd of sheep
arriving in trucks to the hills around our house.
They eat tall grasses to prevent fire.

Newborns baa after their mothers.
Ewes baa back, an octave below the lambs.

We are busy sheltering in place.
No schedules, no outings except to walk.

Only zooming, reading, cleaning,
small trips to the grocery where

we no longer recognize one another.
Masked, gloved, six feet apart.

My daughter and I watch old movies
with low ratings, on television.

We make jokes,
happy to laugh out loud
for the first time in a month.

And I walk in our yard to greet
new roses, Mr. Lincoln, Ingrid Bergman,

Peter Mayle, Cecile Brunner,
old lilacs, and colorful Martha Washington.

They greet me grandly,
show their first best flowers,

pungent smells, tall stalks
healthy in this time of affliction.

Daphne Lifts Up

I bend now so you cannot see my face.
I will touch my toe roots with my silvery
branches, appear to glisten and nod
in consent as you swear love to me.

You will wander twenty years,
wear my soft, sturdy petals,
cook me, eat me, carry me
upon your head.

You will dream of me, I am your tree.
You will see me in Rome with other
conquerors, but you will return here,
a quieter man.

You will sit on my thick feet.
I will rise up tall above you,
reign berries upon you
until you become part of the earth
from which I will grow new fruit.

Gathering and Letting Go

Alone

My soaked knee socks sloshed as I walked in hard rain down Bancroft steps to my first class. My first day at Berkeley, with shiny trees I'd never seen before: Magnolias, Bird of Paradise. Passing stores, names I didn't know: Roos Atkins, Joseph Magnin, dreary, cold, biting rain. Rain at home much softer than this. I glanced up at Sproul Hall, where I was to register.

But at the campus gate, grisly older students in ponchos and jeans. Wet sweatshirts. They must not dress for class. No one carries books.
Hundreds of people shouting, screaming. And blue suited policemen in riot gear. Sticks and guns.

Someone is calling them *Blue Meanies*. Is that from the Beatles album?
The police are hauling students out from the administration building by their hair. Janis, my new roommate, shouting as they drag her into a police van. Why isn't anyone going to class? How can I get through this mass of people? *Can you tell me what's going on?* I ask the woman next to me.
"Where have you been?" she shouts back. "On some desert island?" She turns her back.

A circle forms.
I don't know how to get through the angry crowd. Or around. Better do what seems safer. Do what they do. I hold hands with those closest to me in the circle. They stare at me—must be my knee socks or raincoat. I don't belong. They begin to sing "We Shall Overcome," that new song by Bobby Dylan and Joan Baez. At least I know this from hootenannies. One guy is laughing, points at my penny loafers.

In what underworld am I? I'd rather be on that desert island, with dry socks.

Hello and Good-bye in Athens

Imagining the Acropolis since high school
Latin I, with Mrs. Carfagno.
Statues and boulders of stone everywhere
marble soft and buttery, never in straight lines.

Today, seen in person, early morning sun
with soft shadows alongside the columns.
Tall, steep steps to climb.

The National Museum holds bursting blond statues
strong naked men, chastely dressed women
in flowing gowns. Busts of Hera, Zeus,
of identified and unidentified mortals and gods.

Most striking, family generations, in marble rooms,
showing how good-byes were said.

A woman grieving, her jewel box
handed to her servant,
a man holding an infant out to his dying wife,
A father shaking hands with his young son,
husky horse standing between them.

Room after room full of farewells,
showing death's hello and good-byes.

In Friendship: Anais Nin

I'd carefully planned every word I'd say to Anais when I first met her. The occasion was the Women's Celebration at U.C. Berkeley, December, 1971. I went to see and photograph the writer who most captured my attention when I'd left my husband and lived alone for the first time in my life.

My camera went into action as Anais swept across the stage in her floor-length velvet winter gown. Using no flash at F8 for 1/30th of a second, I wondered if any of the two rolls would print worth anything. I took her as she read, as she spoke, every word elegant, and beautiful to my ears. Her hands fluttered and pointed, as a ballerina. Her voice so soft you had to lean to hear.

She was petite, smaller than I'd imagined, and perfectly formed. She floated above the floor in red velvet, the supple dancer she was trained to be. She appeared to me French, European. She spoke graciously, with great care. One could never imagine her getting angry at anyone. Someone later asked if she got angry and she responded, "Oh yes. And then I wait. It goes away."

I watched her introducing other speakers, saw how she received their information or poetry. Her face smiled receptivity and wisdom. She reflected before she spoke. Never shot from the hip, always praised the best of what others brought to her on stage. I moved to the stage several times, for close-ups. I liked that I didn't believe in flashbulbs. Like Anais, I never wanted to intrude.

When the day-long event was over, I waited nervously while 100 other women spoke to her. After an hour, I thought, "Would she leave suddenly, before we meet?" I was ready, "Anais, my name is Donna and I've read all of your books." But as she smiled up at me, no words came from my mouth. My excitement and anxiety lunged at my voice and I could not speak. Not even a whisper, when it came my turn. Sensing my surprise and frustration, Anais smiled politely, tried to put me at ease. She held my arm. I remember shaking as she shook my larger hand with her softer, smaller one. The soft sweep of her red sleeve did not shake me from my silence. She'd taken my breath away.

Anais signed my program "In friendship" and I nodded my thanks, believing her, crying the entire time. She said I must write to her.

The photographs did come out. Months later I chose what I thought the best one and mailed an 8 x 10 matt print, on my most expensive Portriga Rapid double weight paper, after hours in the darkroom. The photo was a soft focus portrait of her head and neck, her face responsive, all eyes and attentiveness as she spoke to admirers that previous December. I included a letter, told her she's written about all young women's struggle with who they are. That like her 30 years ago, I was now in psychoanalysis, trying to become who I was meant to be, and not somebody my family designed, my former husband ravaged.

Anais wrote back immediately, thanked me for the portrait and asked if I had others. That she needed photographs to give her audiences and could I show her the rest? This time I sent 5 or 6 more images and waited. I still remember sending that package at the Cow Hollow post office in San Francisco on a cold foggy morning before work, after another 24 hours in the darkroom. I wanted them to be perfect. I held onto the brown envelope for a minute before dropping it into the mail slot, flipping the handle a few times as if my life were hanging in the balance.

Anais' second letter was full of thanks and payment, a personal check! She also sent new books, inscribed to "Donna, master of light and shadows." I dissolved. I danced. I flew around my apartment, singing, spinning out onto my balcony and telling all the cars lined up to go "down Lombard, the crookedest street," "I'm an artist. I can even talk!"

Thus began a correspondence and a job, which lasted six years, until Anais' death in 1977, and with her publishers and husband until now. Anais influenced me in all aspects of my deepest self.

I began living in the moment, thoughtfully, not recklessly. I found an Edwardian cottage and decorated it for my taste alone. I took a painting class, one in ballet. Photography and pottery became hobbies. I enjoyed success at work, was promoted to higher positions. I dated many different men, explored my sexuality openly, came to trust reliable people, work choices, commitments.

This was tough in the seventies when everyone on the west coast was doing the same thing and some were not thoughtful. Or clear or honest about themselves. Or sober.

Anais had taught we could love many different men, even on the same day, and I found that this freedom had its limits, yet was most exciting for a short time. It seemed ironic when men later criticized Anais for the same behaviors they practiced all their lives.

Photography classes with Lynette Lehmann and Ruth Bernhard changed my portraits of people. Images became freer, up closer, unabashedly intimate. I began having two and one woman shows and joined two art galleries over the next fifteen years. Over the last fifteen years of publishing my poetry, my book covers are always my photographs. People often regard them as watercolors.

Anais invited me to join her writing groups in Los Angeles. I wanted to go, but my psychoanalyst advised against interrupting my therapy. (He similarly advised against going to London to study with Anna Freud, when I was accepted at her institute). I think he feared I'd become a radical feminist. I complied with his treatment plan, later wondered about his self-interest. I became a feminist anyway.

Anais used my very first photograph of her on the book jacket of her seventh diary.

Time has passed. In recent years I see a resurgence of interest in Anais' diaries and surreal prose. Whether she remains recognized by the literary world is not as important to me as the effect she had on the women of my generation. At her memorial in Los Angeles in 1977, thousands of women spoke to each other about her personal influence on their lives as the new John Williams quartet played on stage. She wrote to us personally. She encouraged us as equals.

Hers was not the edgy language we are told to use today. Hers was the passionate voice of the free spirit. The authentic voice of a liberated heart. I remember waving to her when I happened to be in a New York City apartment, seventh floor, and she happened to be walking to brunch on the alley below, her publisher beside her. She wore a long black cape that swayed behind her. It was as if she flew, near the ground.

Objects Found

When I worked with a young boy whose IQ
was 184 but who could not learn,

he left notes for me tucked in my office couch,
chairs, underneath table legs.

I never saw him hide his pages,
found them later while cleaning.

Taken together, he made
only sense.
We just had to find it.

We sat and put them together, like a puzzle.

I recall Jacques Offenbach died before he finished
his *Tales of Hoffmann*.

After his death in 1980, bits of his endings
were found, pasted together to make a complete score.

When Emily Dickinson died, she left envelopes
and tickets with poems inscribed,

hundreds more in letters to family and friends,
eventually found, now in a book for us.

I like to think that someone cares
about those scraps left behind,

might find and combine,
make a whole story of our never-finished lives.

Swimming with Swallowtail

As I swim laps at the pool
a glint of yellow above me
a ribbon flapping
undulating
sweeping up, sweeping down,
I stop my rhythm to watch its own.

Yellow, white, with black edges
directly over me, scouting the water
or is it my flowered cap in the pool?

Ah, summer's smile, the swallowtail butterfly
invites me to stop at the end of the lane,
for its dance. I am the lucky one.

The butterfly alights on pool's edge
where cement is wet.
I freeze up over this edge, six inches away
as the yellow beauty pauses, prances up and down,
proboscis extended, two legs and an unfolded

tongue touch a puddle of water, each limb as thin
as thread, imitating a dance I saw
in a history of the twenties. Straight legged,
an inch up, then down
for about three minutes. I hold my excited breath.

Its inch-long body the same yellow and black
stripe as its wings, arches its back, eyes up,
then reverses the arch, back down, bounce-bounce
on wet pavement, stop and stretch, wings close
then open as its body arches upward again.

No obvious sense of my presence, only its body.
As I try to find why it stays so long, I see
a slash from wing tip to body on the left side.
Can it fly? Is it gathering strength for flight
to gardens outside the pool fence?

Slowly, up and off it glides, strong, as I exhale,
swooping in its distinct long arcs: up then down.
I've never been this close to grace.

Heroics

She tells me *no heroic measures.*
I ask what they are.
She says no restarting her heart,
using those big snapping pincers.
She signs a paper, puts it in the freezer
between her ice cubes and strawberries.

In the next room she tells my brother
no heroics.
He says *Sure, don't worry—*
What's for dinner?
I hear her tell my sister, who says
We'll all be there, no need to worry.

Mother takes chemicals as the season
changes, suffers thrush, can't talk,
worry, worry, must get the white count up.
Suctioning, shingles, she still asks
if we'd like to dance
as she waves her plastic tubing.

She invites me to lunch at her hospital
bed, pushes peas around with her fork;
they never go into her mouth.

She falls from her bed while the nurse is out
for a smoke, restraints forgotten.
Mom cracks her rib, punctures her lung, lies
on the hospital floor a long time.

She sinks into acute respiratory failure.
We're far away. She turns semi-comatose.
When I get there, I can't see her body
in the bed.

Flattened, she looks like wrinkled sheets
wearing tubes and more I.V. lines.
The doctor asks *shall we intubate?*
while he's writing in a chart about someone else,
his staff standing ready, shake their heads.

Father says *No*. Brother says *I don't know,
maybe yes*. Sister arches her back and leaves
the room. I ask, *Is breath included? Is this heroic?
She only spoke about her heart.*

She Lay Asleep Wearing Oxygen

She lay asleep wearing oxygen,
a narrow river of air holding her
against hospital pillows, sagging.

The nurse and doctor said
"She's in no pain." As if this
were a fine way to die.
"You could use a ventilator
but *we* wouldn't."

Her blood's bad,
she'd only last a few days."

Plenty of bad blood.
But not that bad,
we'd both grown up.
Forgiven.

Three thousand miles between us
until now, we only spoke of hope.
A few days would be enough. How
about a few hours?

The respiratory therapist said
he "might nick her putting the tube down,
that would be a terrible way to die.
Bleeding out," he said.

I held her sixty year-old hand,
rice paper over blue ribbed fans,
smaller than mine, shrinking,
bleeding out, bleeding in.

I walked in circles in her room,
"I love you Mom. Can you
tell me if you want them to put
a breathing tube down for you?"

No nod, no squeeze,
so tied to you, tied to you.

Her breath shallow, eyes closed.
Heart monitor racing, one hundred
twenty-five beats per minute. That's faster
than mine when I run.

Smack in front of us:
fast, hot tempers, spankings, cold shoulders,
"God damn it to hell," as she opened
boiled eggs for breakfast..

Yet coy, a flirt, beckoning us close.
Full-out laugh that tingled her toes,
even entire rooms, confessions
in cloakrooms, all her secrets.

Tight-tied to her children,
yet didn't speak of her cancer,
didn't see the doctor fast for the biopsy,
said it was arthritis.

Her voice on the phone told the other story.
Her laughing voice had an echo, as if spoken from
the end of a long, empty hall.

All the doors off that hall were closed.
I wanted to run toward her, sliding into her legs,
press my face against her thighs
on the brown shiny linoleum in the darkness, yet
we would meet at the end of the hall, like this.

—2—

She did not move. I took her hand,
squeezed gently. "Can you feel me, Mom?"
Eyes still, as untouched open oysters.

She did not move. She lay in her heart.
She did not see me run to the telephone,
page my uncle, her brother, a doctor, in
New Orleans, just as he got off the plane
from Ireland, the place he had to see instead.

He said "Put the tube down," she did not see this,
when her brother called the oncologist,
told him to intubate, carts and plastic tubing everywhere,
did not see the respiratory therapist's hand shake
readying the tube, and my father shout,
"No more treatment, she's had enough."

Mom didn't see the doctor scream at us, "You people
don't know what you want, from now on I'm going
to tell you—"
or me say, "Doctor, I know this is as hard
for you as it is for us, but some of us haven't seen our mother
and hoped to say good-bye…"

(Where the fuck were you anyway, telling
us we had three months and we've had one?
Because your nurses didn't watch her, she fell,
punctured her lung with the broken rib. Where
were you, doctor?)

Nor could she watch the yards of tubing tripping us,
the shaken staff slink out of the room with the family.

I held her hand, fingered her worn wedding ring,
told her we were all around her and she could do
what she needed to do, that we would not leave.

Her ring, worn thin, had no more edges,
almost seemed part of her finger.
I worried that I could rub it away.

She had rubbed me away so well,
Camille at stage center, me in the wings.
I was glad to be away to grow up, until now.

Blood trickled from her nose, I patted
this stream with my fingers, forgetting
where I was. The heart monitor
flashed one-hundred-forty.

Bright red trickle, stream from her heart.
I thought of bloody knees, mercurochrome,
menstruation, the hat she wore to the movie
in the gym for fifth grade girls, rivers,
how she swam only sidestroke,
rivulets, how her supple skin
looked like thirty, always young, she would
never grow lines, her heart
running her life like a river, overflowing its banks.

—3—

Mother lifted her head all at once.
Blue eyes open, moving to alert,
looked at me and smiled,

raised her hand to form the shape
of the two zebras on the last card I'd sent,
her mouth formed "little horse."

I smiled with her, our eyes meeting.
She could not speak but pointed
to her ribs, where she was broken.

"Yes, you fell, you broke your rib.
Does it hurt?" (They didn't catch you,
they forgot. I will sue.)
She shook her head fast, like a little girl in a hurry.
Showing me everything, as if in a dream, went on to
something else, as if we were sharing tea on her
wrought-iron patio table in Mayfield.

She mouthed my name, "Donna," four times.
I wasn't sure at first, since she made no sound.
"Donna." She paused between each utterance,

as if she wanted to be sure I heard.
"Donna." She wasn't in a hurry. She seemed certain.
"I'm here, Mom….yes."
In slow motion, her head up then down, " D o n n a……"

Why my streaming eyes took in her toes then, spread with those
sponge things, I don't know.
She'd had a pedicure last night.

I lay my hand on her arm, placed
her hand in my two.
Her head sunk to her chest.
The others arrived like walking corpses.
We stood around her in a circle
while her heart raced higher.

—4—

She'd written in her journal
"When I die, I'd like
my family around me in a circle one last time. I'd look
into each of their eyes and say, "It's been
a three ring circus, Barnum and Bailey all the way."

She could not speak these words.
I kept saying, "We're all here, Mom, we're around you."
My brother and I leaned into each other, like frozen life rafts.
.
We watched her sinking, sinking.
I wanted to tear out my heart and give it to her.

We were all drowning. Her breath stopped.
My father seemed to recede into his clothes.
My sister sang East Indian prayers for crossing over.
I wondered if they comforted Mom, who never liked them.
Her heart stopped. The green line flat, flat, flat (I wanted
to smash the machine, crash it on the nurses who did not watch her).

Mother seemed to grow smaller into her pillows.
Her body in the same posture when she gave us birth.

Legs spread, toes ready.
No more blood, only tears covering us like a river.

—5—

The others rushed out, exhausted.
The nurse "cleaned her up," moved her
to a small white room with cold concrete walls.
She needed no cleaning. She smelled soft and warm.

I held her hand, still heated,
felt her still there, still young,
her brow relaxed, her breathing
no longer labored.
She'd hate to be alone in a place like this.

I told her she fought well, she was beautiful,
that I would always love her and remember everything.
I wondered if I should take her ring, looser now.
No. She'd want to wear it at a time like this.

Her hand grew cooler, I rubbed it a little,
wanted to warm her, found my hand running
up her arm to her cheek, fighting panic.
From the beginning, her skin.

I felt she was still there, if not in her heart,
then in the air-cold room.

A thin circle of light reflected
on the white hospital wall
from the early October sunset.

It grew smaller and smaller.
I waited, singing lullabies
until it went out.

Sarah Mae

She jumped up from her kitchen table
when her husband whispered, "English."

As he slowly let us into their boot room
I watched her dash to the only bedroom,
pull up the tattered blue coverlet over
a pillow's edge—her own bed,
low to the ground, shared with the quiet
fringed-chin man who let us in.

She shushed her girls, two in cotton bonnets,
hers in chiffon, ties hanging down.
The girls swept their gray dresses to the next
room, peered out at us from a half-closed door.
I peeked at them as they glimpsed me.

We walked across a dark, long-paneled floor.
It could have been a dancing floor. No furniture
in this room, just four hand-hewn rocking chairs
lined bare walls. And an old open Bible, on a stand.

I smiled into a soft kindness, Sarah Mae's face,
as she lifted out the quilts. Half were Amish,
deep colors against black ground, half were what
she imagined we'd like:
white and lavender gingham, pale peony flowers,
purples and blues. All sizes, colors, patterns:
wedding ring and sunburst. I tried hard to
just look at the quilts, but my eyes traveled to
her sweet full mouth, her hushed children,
swinging around the door, holding its porcelain knob,
to her treasure chest full of hand-sewn cloth, waiting for us.

Nine Years After Mom Died

You gave as much as you took away. I can say that now,
all of it pressed together, mixed up, tossed, like salad,
a very big salad with chocolate chips, name-calling,
delight, derision, and other mysteries thrown in.

You kept on giving, after we both grew up,
even with the interstices where your pain once held me.
You gave beyond reason, beyond pain, behind hurt, beyond life.

I sat in your private room where October cold crawled.
Your young body slumped against pillows. No breath left. Nor hurt.
In the dark room the others had fled. I held your hand.
Your hand, still warm. You seemed lonely. You were still there.

Autumn light streamed through the streaked windows.
Onto your young soft skin, skin never to know old age.
While my streaming tears could not save you, or my staying.
Or my fierce will.

Your love spread around me there, on the sheets.
Your soul inhabited that space between the sun's light.
And my cold shaken frame.

Perhaps some of it entered me,
lasting to this day.
For I hold you very close.
Fondly,
and am still kissed by your keen sensibilities
and full blown laugh.

Old Faithful
       Yellowstone National Park

The gathered people wait.
Hold themselves upright,
then reach forward
with backs and necks pulling
them from their benches, like pews
at the second Easter Sunday
service, not sure what
to expect.
Someone asks, "Has she started yet?"

And then she does.
Sputters, a trickle.
Everyone laughs, jittery.

Then higher, a stream, pointed
straight up, each gust
a little higher, then more
gallons spurting skyward.

Now they all sigh or laugh,
And those who haven't seen
her before think it's over.
Some depart their chosen
spots, not knowing
she's just begun.

Only the faithful, those
who join her water, reach higher
with her, feel her spray, feel
the force of the weight of her
building higher, spreading,
cascading out.

And the white water, so wide
and elemental, some open
their mouths and say

 "Ah—oh—yes—*look at her go*

Water forced from under the ground tumbles,
splatters knees and feet,
children's bare legs.
Everyone who stays,
happier than they thought possible,
thrilled even, not sure why, smiling.

Reunion: Winter Visit, Family Homestead

We trudge up the dirt road from the new house with all the kids. It's been five winters since our families arrive together on the hill. Jared and Chris take the lead, Will and Juliet a few paces behind. We older ones, brother and sister who form the canopy over the rest, are happy to walk at the back of the parade. The way our parents did forty years ago after the fire. Snow covers the road and the long grass of the old lawn. We leave the road and walk the two hundred yards, hand-in-hand to steady ourselves, to the foundation of the old house.

We're excited because the winter allows us to get closer to the stones than we could in summer. The trees arch over the spot but don't get in our way. Saplings have grown in the kitchen, the bathroom, right where my cousin chased me with the snake until I screamed, from the toilet seat.

How small the frame looks. Not quite a rectangle. More like three rectangles and a square, as additions were put in place. The kitchen got bigger, the back bedroom was put on, the front porch of brick. Some in 1914 when Grandma and Grandpa came here as newlyweds, some in the twenties when the depression forced the family of six back to the farm. The cherry tree still stands out back. The six maples, now gnarly and dying, still line the lawn in front.

Now stars of snowflakes cover the stacked field stones. The outline of a house once ten rooms large. The kids pop over the top, jump into what used to be the dirt floor of Grandma's home, the Dascomb Aerie. The place we lived in for every vacation of our childhoods.

"Here's where the kitchen came up," my brother announces. "Now where was the stair down to the basement?"

"Right to your right, beside the old green and cream wood stove. Remember? Grandpa used to lift the door right out of the floor," We laugh.

"Well then, this must be the door to the back porch, where Pook and Pookie sunned themselves," brother Ralph continues.

"Yes and over here is the door to your and Alan's room, next to the wood burning stove," I remind him. "And Sherry and I slept right here, with Grandma and Grandpa, next to you. The porch door is over there," I point.

"How could all of those rooms fit on such a small foundation?" Chris asks.

That's how we begin the story again. Sitting on the stones of the house, some by the kitchen, some of us on the front room side, the youngest in the basement, on flat, stacked rocks in December.

On the Plaza, Santa Fe

First, her dusky eyes,
rounded almonds, brown as earth.

Her black hair shines, hangs long
behind her soft neck.

"This is my first day, here...
These are my own designs..."

She sweeps her brave hand across
mosaics of turquoise, jasper, jet,
gaspeite, gold.

New shapes, modern composition.

I want to buy her jewelry,
tell her she tells the truth
and betrays no one.

I want to tuck her eyes
into my pockets.

In the Blue Room

Wound tight and tired, he sat us down
around his formica kitchen table,
as if for a meeting of his board:
ready to announce his funeral plans.

He spoke with such authority
I almost didn't register the sheer white terror
behind his glassy blue eyes.

Then, tucking him in after his first surgery,
alone in that blue-cold room, no nurse nearby,
he whispered, fingers reaching my wrist:

"I think I'm going to beat this thing, honey!"

The doctor would tell him the next day
what he had just told me,
of the oat cell cancer
and three months to live.
But Dad's boy-hope bloomed like a balloon
that glowing night
bouncing about his room for the last time.

Dad, it's good to see you happy.
We'll take this one step at a time.

We squeezed hands. I'd never tucked
my father into bed before. I folded each
corner, the way he taught me, military style,
pulled the cloth as high as it could go,
firm against his big chest, lingering
over the cotton.

Lampyridae

As I walk down the June steps
of the farmhouse, not quite silent
fireflies flash close to my face.

Droplets of light fill the night sky,
small lights coming toward me,
bobbling, dipping down, as far as I can see.

A brushing against my hair, a clicking sound
near the ground you have to care to hear.

We used to catch them in jars, sit them
next to our beds until their lights went out.
Or pound nail holes in the jar tops so they'd
stay with us till morning.

Mating time, the males flashing, the females
close to the ground on the grass blades,
the bushes. If the lights grow closer together,
all is well for the next generation.

One large lightning bug
tries to come into our bedroom
window, knocking on the pane.
The room fills full with his clicking

sound and light, magnified by window glass.
He lightens our faces like a bright candle,
softening bedposts
and our startled eyes.

The Changing Season

Yesterday, summer scalded us.
Today, morning bursts of cold.
Billows of cumulus overhead
lope across a cornflower sky.

Red and orange trees drop ready leaves
into upsweeps of sudden breeze.
Yesterday we voted for a new president.
Today he begins to lead.

As I drive through new green after rain,
Beethoven's Seventh Symphony fills me.
Timpani deep, resonant behind building chords,
cheerful horns, all the seated and standing strings.

Fluttering violins start to mute years of pain
allow layers of protection to loosen.

This almost full year of widespread pandemic,
keeping us apart from family and touch,
pushed our bodies to shrivel, shrink, crouch.

Today expansive music accompanies the election,
opens our closed selves, urges me to stretch, unfold, reach.

In my driveway, the symphony's last movement pulls me up
from my seat, legs somehow strong, reaching to the grass,
arms above me,
spread until dancing violins take me to calm courage.

Dance for thoughtful leadership! Dance for reunions of
children with their parents along our southern border.
Dance for the return of care for the earth and sky.
No more elephant trophy hunting,
no mining in the National Forests,
new protections for violated Alaskan open space.

Twirl for a cabinet of many colors.
Embrace the return to our allies, the Paris Accord.

Shout out for the all-night vote counters, pats for
the new young voters, those suppressed in Georgia
for a century. Clap for people of color
dancing in Philadelphia, people of all colors opening
their doors to bright sun and a President-elect
who carries mercy and understanding in his arms.

Virginia and Juliet

The two wrap arms around each other,
one celebrating youth's dazzle as well as this day,
the other helping her grandmother
stand up, not minding the weight.

Virginia and Juliet stand together
where the new Louisville bridge spans
the restless Ohio River. The Seneca called
the Ohio "Good River." Everyone's allowed
to cross the old bridge next to it on foot one more time.

The older woman in her ninth decade has crossed
this bridge all her life.
The younger in her second decade of life
has never seen this bridge, this lively river.
She likes to walk and run,
loves Virginia as grandmother.

They both speak of the classical music piped in
along the struts of the bridge.
You can hear it all the way across to Indiana!

Virginia reminds Juliet, *Ohio hails from the Iroquois.*
Iroquois and Shawnee as well as pioneers
on their way west paddled their canoes here.

They smile at each other as big as the broad Ohio,
border to five states, at its widest here, a mile across.

Arm-in-arm, singing the names of a dozen tributaries,
Monongahela, Allegheny, Little Muskingum…
Virginia and Juliet promenade the span.

Porcelain Cups in the Sun

I love brown horses rolling on their backs in a field of dirt, clouds of dust billowing above them.

And cows running downhill, rocking see-saw, pushed forward by their heavy heads, so both back legs push up off the ground at the same time.

I love fog over Mill Valley at four o'clock before it knows it's fog. Triple rainbows in Glacier or any rainbow anywhere when people stop and point, unable to carry on.

I love poets who forget their own work and really listen to another poet read, never once leaving the poem.

I love classes where students love learning so much they enter in, transcend with you, fly near the ceiling and say *Oh ... Yes ... Of course ... And ...*

I love hummingbirds whirring among the branches who slow down, letting you see them or let you talk to them or don't see you standing frozen there.

And girls at ten who smile like that girl over there, open eyed, open mouthed at her grandmother's story and grandfather's smile.

I love porcelain cups in the sun, staunch in their perfect reflections.

Birdsong

She spent two days with birds before her last surgery.
After the chemo, radiation, talk of mother's three
cancer sites. She walked the levees in Cosumnes.

Talked to the white fronts, kingfishers, cinnamon teals.
Not about her decision against reconstruction,
or even her terror of what was to come.

Listened for the snow geese: was it too late?
Had they already scattered?
Searched off the main roads, back in the farmers'

ponds, wanting their chattering, their fly-ups,
a curtain of opals to sweep her clean
with wing flutter, see them swoop down

each one finding a perfect spot among
the others, without a squawk. To rest.

Flocks learn fifty calls from their parents, she tells me.
When they fly, they listen to other neighborhoods
of birds to see if they belong.

The closer the male and female are
in color, the more likely they'll mate for life.
Otherwise it's just for the season.

The only birds who can smell are the buzzards.
She admires their work. They are the nurses.

She told me she didn't think she'll die
this week, but if she does, she's filled herself
with birdsong, skeins of snow geese flying at dusk.

Blood Appears

At the new International Corning Glass Museum I walked fast
to the women's room, feeling an uncommon urgency.
Mild cramping, weak walk.

There I saw blood for the first time in many years.
I smiled like I used to,
every month, being one of those girls who wore menstruation
like a badge of courage.

What red used to mean was an egg, my egg, traveling bravely down
my fallopian tubes, swiveling her hips a little, awaiting
just one sperm or the entire pool, or not caring at all,
dedicated to her own destiny.

Even glad in my twenties, when it meant I wasn't pregnant,
tubing down the Snake River, when blood flowed unexpectedly,
running down both legs as I climbed out of cold water,
and the boy I was with thought I'd cut myself on a rock
while I ran fast to a latrine for toilet paper.

At the museum, I said my postmenopausal age aloud.
That wiped away my smile because I had to take one of
life's worst next steps: calling the doctor.
Doctors always ask if you know where the blood came from.

Enter Autumn

This season of ripening, weaving threads together
letting them go

My mother's best friend died today.
Her brother died two years ago
on this same day
Mother died in this same week thirty-three years before

I sit now to recover breath on this grey bench
inhale nature, return to it.

Next to me, soft trumpet flower announces endings

Blows its horn, wind does the rest.
Yellow landings, stems fall, slide into soil
as they reach the old garden
Broad leaves green until their brown curling.

Abundant life requires savor, settling, middles,
fingering edges, brims, even ragged rims, empty corners.

Inside and Out

Inside

While the farmhouse stood on the hill,
ten wall-papered rooms on two floors,
we slept inside.

Cousins in five bedrooms with chamber pots.
Aunt Liva's quilts, Aunt Sarah's squeaky beds,
a wood burning stove in the dining room below.

All chores shared, taking food for pigs, cows, horses
as well as a dozen of us staying the summer.

First summer, planting pipes underground for water.
Raspberries in the garden, jelly and jam in June.

Until the water ran, we boiled it from the well.
Used a chair with cane seat cut-out
to go to the far garden 'bathroom.'

Second summer, learning all about horses,
with Jenny and Doughboy. Every day a new trail.

We lived on the hilltop: a long dirt road in, longer
dusty road out. The road holds our family name in its
dust and stones. In its sleeves, cornflower, Queen Anne's lace.

Outside

After the house burned down, we camped
on the land near the house's foundation.
The grass long and shiny.

Birds woke us up. Wind breathed us to sleep.
We cooked on long tables we made, by the pond,
fished for bass and blue gill.

No matter whether house or lawn held us,
we walked at midnight, with the same
Milky Way, at dawn with chickadee and wren.

Nests of birds we knew—we still imitate their calls,
near meadows ringed with maple, oak and birch.
Bush of blackberry, sprig of strawberry,

apple orchard near the hemlock barn.
Connected to mother, grandfather, rows of family.
County Steuben, country churches, neighbors waving.

Sleeping out connected us to bird and frog, fireflies,
damselfly, butterfly, family of deer, one black bear.

A long dirt road in, a longer dusty road out.
The road holds our family name in its dust and stones.
In its sleeves, cornflower and Queen Anne's lace.

What I Want to Know

The gravel beds are gone
to build our homes and bridges
where the gray and pink fish
used to lay their eggs.

The Russian River's shadowy inlets
where the salmon rested
have been straightened out.

What I want to know is
when the last Coho salmon
are placed in their streams,
can they get back home?

And if these sleek fish know
only hatchery life, they've lost
their navigational compass anyway.

When my daughter's fourth grade class
visited the Iron Gate hatchery,
the girls could only cry and hold
their stomachs, watching the men squeeze
the Coho's abdomen for eggs,
then toss her into a chute.

What I want to know is why France can
separate waterways for fish and wineries
while we mix all together,
ensuring salmon's decline?

The Pomo say
they never taught their salmon
to climb ladders.

The Dascomb Aerie

I lift the old wooden fold-out chair from the shed. Its canvas cover is faded. I can still make out stripes of orange, yellow, red, with a thin line of royal blue every now and then.

We walk, the chair and I, to the mound of soft grass where the house used to be. The grass under my feet is long and shiny. It feels as it did in the 1950's when we sat under these same maple trees, now as then fluttering in the breeze.

I can still see aunts and uncles strewn about on cotton quilts here, near the old house. They talk about fishing, going gliding later today, about Eisenhower and that oddball Nixon. They laugh, telling the story of splashing in Campbell Creek below the farm when they were kids. They had one bathing suit among the four of them and had to give it to the minister's son, who came along.

They take in summer sun, rolling leg on leg, rubbing on sun tan lotion, grooming each other. My Dad and Uncle Cecil, shirtless, boxer shorts showing above bermudas, lying on their stomachs. Mom and Aunt Jane, hair pulled back with combs and rubber bands, slide their oiled hands up and down their husbands' backs. Other than here, I don't see men lying down like this, close as all four in bed together. Other than here, my father never lies down, except at night. Uncle John sits in his yellow polo shirt and shorts, sucking on his pipe, while Aunt Betty slaps a fly on her soft knee. Harry's at the pond with the boys, fishing. Aunt Helen's gone shopping in Hornell.

Waves of heat, flush with red raspberry smell, move over us. Grandpa's leaning down in the berry patch, in his sleeveless ribbed grey undershirt and grey post office pants, a two gallon metal pail on his belt, picking berries. We'll have them for dinner and breakfast, then lunch too. We girls will help our moms can them in jellies tomorrow.

I follow the thick, drunk flight of bumblebees on the cluster of thistle flowers next to Grandma's lawn chair. She says, "When we were kids we used to make hot pads out of these. See how the thorns hold them together? They were real pretty." She and I put thistle flowers together to make pads for the family dinner table.

The Cows on Our Street

Seven cows lie in the sun at the end of our street,
beside the red barn: Black Angus, caramel-colored Jersey.

They ruminate and loll in earth's warmth,
accustomed to me sitting there on the fence.

The creamy one I call Buttercup sniffs toward me
then rotates her head as if to give me her full view.
She's pooched out, expecting a calf next month.

When I return two hours later
the herd stands up the far hill grazing.

They go there to eat greener grass.
Their going allows me to go too.
Until Buttercup's bell sounds.

They form a line to the barn.

Cows running downhill, calves kicking up their heels,
my favorite part.

Belting Out Beethoven

I sing Beethoven's Seventh Symphony as I drive home,
try to land the notes.
All of Beethoven's symphonies perfect for belting out
during the pandemic, the continuation of pandemic,
spikes in our two year pandemic.

Wild horses come to mind in the second half,
running in the sand dunes in North Carolina,
the way they used to run in Nevada, fast and free,
hair blowing wide from tail and mane,
over mounds. The tympani sound out
their heartbeats, almost as one.
Safe in their numbers, their usual path, sometimes touching.

I sing because I saw an old, fast friend, who understood
all I said, and I heard her. We didn't want to part,
so we kept walking. We saw a toddler from another country
walking with her mother, and we all smiled together.
We said "You are walking!" Her mother said "Marche! Marche!"
—the baby smiled and kept walking.

I sing because egrets were flying and landing
in the small creek puddles of water at the park.
The blue tolerated the snowy and the great.
There was room enough for all to go fishing.
A fish for every bird.

Acknowledgments

Avatar Review: "Hello and Good-bye in Athens," 2021

Brief Wilderness: "Unraveling," 2021

Cape Rock Journal: "In the Middle of a Long Marriage," 2019

Chaffin: "Mildred Belle," 2014, "Listening to *L'Isle Joyeuse*," 2021

Chicago Quarterly Review: "Vernal Sap," "Mystery of the Boil," 2020

COG Magazine: "After Winter Rains," 2019

Crone, Women Coming of Age: "She Lay Asleep Wearing Oxygen," 2008

Door is a Jar: "What I Want to Know," 2018

Evening Street Review: "On the Lakeshore Limited," 2019, "Virginia and Juliet," 2023, "The Changing Season," 2023

Front Range Review: "The Cows on Our Street," 2021

Gemini: "Before AIDS Was a Word," 2010, nominated for a Pushcart; nominated for Best of the Net, 2012

Grasslimb: "Heroics," 2009

Grub Street Review: "The Dascomb Aerie," 2021

The Healing Muse: "In the Retelling," 2019, "Ask Her" (as "Belle XII"), 2020, "In the Blue Room," 2021, "Enter Autumn," 2022

Lips: "Gustav Klimt," 2021

The London Magazine: "For Mary, *Sotto Voce*," 2017

Louisiana Literature: "Inside and Out," 2021

MacGuffin: "Living Language," 2019

Magnolia Review: "After Winter Rains (R)," "In the Dark," 2020

Marin Poetry Anthology: "A Boy Named Ned," 2018, "Long Distance," 2019 nominated for a Pushcart, "Belting Out Beethoven," 2022

Outrider Press: "Birdsong," 2022

Paterson Literary Review: "I Was Raised on Love," 2022, "Reunion: Winter Visit, Family Homestead," 2022, "Sarah Mae," Editor's Choice Poem for Allen Ginsberg Contest, 2023, published 2024

Poetry Letter: "Canada Goose Nesting," 2007

Praxis: Journal of Gender and Cultural Critiques: "At Four and Thirty," 2022, "Porcelain Cups in the Sun," 2009

Schuylkill Valley Journal of the Arts: "Hummingbird Couple," 2006

Spotlong Review: "On the Plaza, Santa Fe," 2022

The Summerset Review: "Skimming the Water," 2019

Ship of Fools: "Daphne Lifts Up," 2009

Tiferet, A Journal of Spiritual Literature: "In Friendship: Anais Nin," 2017

Weber: the Contemporary West: "A Day's Work," 2020, "Before Mother Died," 2020, "Objects Found," 2023

Westview: "Lampyridae," 2019

"After Winter Rains" was anthologized in *The Freedom of New Beginnings, Poems of Witness and Vision from Sonoma County, California,* Phyllis Meshulam, Editor, 2022

Many thanks to those readers and writers who listened and offered wisdom for my third full-length collection of poems: my reading groups with Ron Thomas, Helen Heal, Gail Calvello, Godelieve Uyttenhove, Lynn Camhi, Geri diGiorno.

Gratitude for reflecting with me about Daphne: Elizabeth Herron, Barbara Marlin, Susan Bono.

Thank you to my husband for his patient technical help as well as my children, who critiqued poems as well as the covers of *Daphne Lifts Up*.

About the Author

Donna writes on both coasts, divides her year between New York and California. In so doing, she keeps close contact with all of her children, cousins, her 101 year- old aunt. Returning to her maternal grandmother's homestead, she finds inspiration in the four seasons and wildlife from her childhood. California provides much natural inspiration as well. Her grandson shows her new vantage points, every week.

Returning to the study of classical piano has brought new sounds and textures to her writing.

She continues to publish poems, creative nonfiction, and memoir. Since her second full- length collection she has garnered another nomination for a Pushcart, and a 2023 Editor's Choice award from the Alan Ginsberg contest. She has published regularly with *Evening Street Review, Weber: the Contemporary West, The Healing Muse, the Chaffin Journal, Marin Poetry Anthology, Paterson Literary Review, Praxis,* and *Louisiana Literature*. Some of these journals have published multiple poems as special features.

Anthologies showing her work include *Fire and Rain: Ecopoetry of California* and *The Freedom of New Beginnings, Poems of Witness and Vision from Sonoma County, California*. Her prose piece "Maid of Cotton," in both English and Spanish, appeared in *La Presa*, Spring, 2024.

Donna enjoys her ongoing poetry readings on both coasts. She continues her membership in the Marin Poetry Center where she served for several years as Events Chair and on the Board. Recently she has been asked by editors of poetry journals to judge annual contests. See her website for new work and her ongoing reading schedule: donnaemerson.com.

www.ingramcontent.com/pod-product-compliance
Lightning Source LLC
Chambersburg PA
CBHW030053170426
43197CB00010B/1510